WHO WE ARE

THE ASIAN AMERICAN EXPERIENCE

Andrea C. Nakaya

San Diego, CA

About the Author

Andrea C. Nakaya, a native of New Zealand, holds a BA in English and an MA in communications from San Diego State University. She has written and edited numerous articles and more than fifty books on current issues. She currently lives in Eagle, Idaho, with her husband and their two children, Natalie and Shane.

© 2023 ReferencePoint Press, Inc.
Printed in the United States

For more information, contact:
ReferencePoint Press, Inc.
PO Box 27779
San Diego, CA 92198
www.ReferencePointPress.com

ALL RIGHTS RESERVED.
No part of this work covered by the copyright hereon may be reproduced or used in any form or by any means—graphic, electronic, or mechanical, including photocopying, recording, taping, web distribution, or information storage retrieval systems—without the written permission of the publisher.

LIBRARY OF CONGRESS CATALOGING-IN-PUBLICATION DATA

Names: Nakaya, Andrea C., 1976- author.
Title: The Asian American experience / by Andrea C. Nakaya.
Description: San Diego : ReferencePoint Press, Inc., [2023] | Series: Who we are | Includes bibliographical references and index.
Identifiers: LCCN 2022030052 (print) | LCCN 2022030053 (ebook) | ISBN 9781678204662 (library binding) | ISBN 9781678204679 (ebook)
Subjects: LCSH: Asian Americans--History--Juvenile literature. | Asian Americans--Social conditions--Juvenile literature. | Asian Americans--Ethnic identity--Juvenile literature.
Classification: LCC E184.A75 N35 2023 (print) | LCC E184.A75 (ebook) | DDC 305.895/073--dc23/eng/20220629
LC record available at https://lccn.loc.gov/2022030052
LC ebook record available at https://lccn.loc.gov/2022030053

CONTENTS

Asian Americans: By the Numbers   **4**

Introduction   **6**
A Diverse Group of People

Chapter One   **10**
Asian Immigration to the United States

Chapter Two   **20**
Fighting for Rights

Chapter Three   **29**
Creating New Communities

Chapter Four   **38**
Embracing Identity

Chapter Five   **47**
Ongoing Challenges

Source Notes   56
For Further Research   59
Index   61
Picture Credits   64

ASIAN AMERICANS: BY THE NUMBERS

Total Population
- 19.9 million identify as Asian American alone
- 4.1 million identify as Asian American in combination with another ethnic group

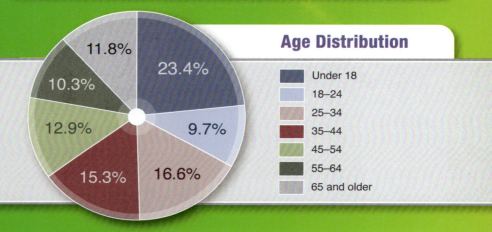

Age Distribution
- Under 18: 23.4%
- 18–24: 9.7%
- 25–34: 16.6%
- 35–44: 15.3%
- 45–54: 12.9%
- 55–64: 10.3%
- 65 and older: 11.8%

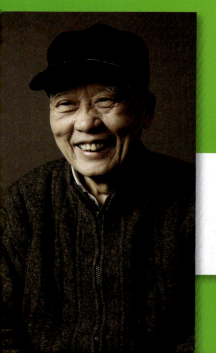

Education
- High school diploma: 87.8%
- Bachelor's degree: 55.6%
- Graduate or professional degree: 24.7%

Life Expectancy
- For both men and women, 80.7 years
- For women, 82.7 years
- For men, 78.4 years

Six Largest Origin Groups

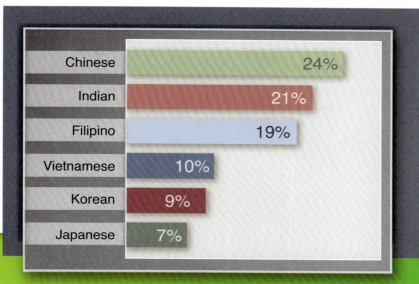

- Chinese 24%
- Indian 21%
- Filipino 19%
- Vietnamese 10%
- Korean 9%
- Japanese 7%

Median Household Income

- $93,759

Five States with Largest Asian American Populations

INTRODUCTION

A Diverse Group of People

As part of a 2021 series on Asian American identity, journalist Karen Turner interviewed a number of different people who call themselves Asian American. She spoke to Nicole Chung, who was born in Seattle and raised in southern Oregon. "I'm Korean American and my adoptive family is white," Chung told her. "Around the time that I was growing up . . . I . . . did not actually get to know or become close with any fellow Korean Americans." Eric Nguyen grew up in a suburb of Washington, DC, and told Turner that he was surrounded by Asian Americans who were well-off and had been in the United States for generations. However, he added, "My parents were immigrants who did manual labor and were more comfortable speaking Vietnamese." Turner also spoke to Diksha Basu, who moved to the United States while in middle school and continues to take regular trips back to India. Basu explained, "I divide my time between India and America, fortunate enough to be able to call both home."[1] These are just three examples of how *Asian American* can mean many different things. There are millions of Asian Americans living in the United States, and each one of them has a different story.

Many Different Experiences

Asian Americans can trace their origins back to a wide variety of countries. The US Census Bureau—which regularly collects data about the US population—defines Asian as "a person having origins in any of the original peoples of the Far East, Southeast Asia, or the Indian subcontinent including, for example, Cambodia, China, India, Japan, Korea, Malaysia, Pakistan, the Philippine Islands, Thailand, and Vietnam."[2] In 2020 the US Census Bureau found that there are almost 20 million people in the United States who identify as Asian alone, and another 4.1 million who identify as Asian in combination with another racial group. The Pew Research Center also collects population data. It reports that Asian Americans can have roots in more than twenty different countries, each with its own unique culture and history. According to Pew, the largest Asian American groups in the United States are Chinese American, Indian American, and Filipino American; however, the center says that no one Asian ethnicity makes up a majority.

Those people who identify as Asian American also have extremely diverse stories about why they or their ancestors came to the United States. There are refugees fleeing war or persecution, parents in search of better economic opportunities for their families, students working toward degrees from US schools, families looking to escape crowded cities, wealthy investors establishing second homes, people who want to join their families already in the United States, and many more unique experiences. Some of these individuals had no trouble immigrating to the United States, while others had to wait years for permission to do so. A significant percentage entered the country illegally; according to the Pew Research Center, about 14 percent of the unauthorized immigrants in the United States come from Asia.

In addition to diverse origin stories, Asian Americans also have a wide variety of different experiences of life in the United States. For instance, some report that they have encountered racism and discrimination, while others say they have not. There are Asian Americans who are still becoming accustomed to US culture, and others who were born in the United States and have never even traveled to any Asian country. Many Asian Americans have a strong connection to their Asian heritage, but others know very little about their Asian culture.

Indian Americans (pictured) make up the second-largest Asian American group in the United States after Chinese Americans.

Difficult to Define

As a result of such diversity, *Asian American* is not an easy thing to define. Photojournalist Jonathan Frydman also spoke to a number of different Asian Americans about identity—all of them young people living in Los Angeles—and, like Turner, he found an incredible variety of stories. After hearing all of these stories, Frydman concluded:

> "Asian American" is one of those impossibly complex, fluctuating terms. It's used to define some 23 million people living in the United States . . . whose families have roots in countries ranging from the Philippines to India to North Korea. The umbrella term is meant to encompass recent immigrants and people whose families have lived in the U.S. for generations, not to mention people with incredibly varied cultures, histories, languages, and religions.[3]

8

As a result of such variation, some people argue that it makes no sense to group so many people together under the term *Asian American*. They point out that many members of that group seem to have nothing in common.

Yet even though there is great diversity among Asian Americans, shared experiences are not uncommon. Erika Lee is the granddaughter of Chinese immigrants. In her book *The Making of Asian America: A History*, Lee discusses the diversity and shared experiences when she says:

> There is great diversity within Asian America and across Asian American history, but there are also significant similarities and connections. For instance, many Asian American immigrants have faced similar challenges in negotiating an identity that includes both Asia and the United States. Others have had to face discrimination and stereotypes, simply because of the way that they look.[4]

As Lee concludes, understanding what it means to be Asian American means embracing both these shared experiences and also the many differences that are found in the Asian American story. It is this rich and complex identity that makes Asian Americans who they are.

"There is great diversity within Asian America and across Asian American history, but there are also significant similarities and connections."[4]

—Erika Lee, the granddaughter of Chinese immigrants

CHAPTER ONE

Asian Immigration to the United States

Chinese immigrants were one of the first groups to come from Asia to the United States in significant numbers. Like most early immigrants, they came in search of economic opportunity. Erika Lee explains, "Labor recruiters in China bombarded prospective immigrants with the message that, as one advertisement proclaimed, 'Americans are very rich people. They want the Chinaman to come. . . . Money is in great plenty and to spare in America.'"[5] She says that there were sixty-three thousand Chinese people in the United States by 1870. Many of them did find the opportunities they were looking for, making enough money to support families back in China or start their own businesses.

However, not all Americans were as welcoming as advertised. No matter how hard they worked or how much they contributed to society, many early Chinese immigrants were treated with hostility and racism. One example of that is the Chinese immigrants who helped build the transcontinental railroad, which connected the West and East Coasts of the United States. Without their hard work, that railroad would not have been completed. However, many of those workers were treated as inferior and unwanted. Helen Zia, a journalist and author of *Asian American Dreams*, says, "The Chinese workers shoveled, picked, blasted, and drilled their way through boulders, rock, and dirt, often suspended from mountain peaks high in the Sierras, even in the harsh mountain winters."[6] According to her research, an estimated one in ten died from the harsh working conditions. However, when the railroad was finished in 1869, the contributions of these men were ignored. Zia says that they were excluded from the grand opening of the railroad and not even allowed to ride on it. However, despite being treated so unfairly, immigrants continued to travel to the United States from China and many other Asian countries, beginning in the 1800s and continuing today. These immigrants have had a variety of experiences. Many have enjoyed success, but just as many have been subjected to racist treatment and restrictions of rights.

Early Chinese Immigrants

Like the railroad workers, most early Asian immigrants to the United States worked as laborers. During the 1800s the United States was growing rapidly and needed cheap labor in a variety of industries, including mining, railroad construction, farming, fishing, and factories. Many Asian immigrants were willing to take these jobs and to do them for lower pay than other people. The Asia Society stresses the importance of early Asian immigrants to the United States. It says, "Asian immigrants have played a vital role in the development of this country."[7] The majority of these early immigrants were men. Most intended to stay only temporarily in the United States, saving money and then returning home, but some later sent for their families and stayed permanently. The first immigrants went to Hawaii, where they worked as agricultural laborers on plantations. Soon after that, large numbers of Asian immigrants began to go to the West Coast of the United States.

Despite the need for immigrant laborers, many Americans disliked having a large number of Asians in their communities. They crafted laws to stop more from coming and to restrict those who were there already. The first laws targeted Chinese immigrants. For example,

"Asian immigrants have played a vital role in the development of this country."[7]

—Asia Society, a nonprofit organization that works to educate the world about Asia

In the 1800s, Chinese immigrants helped build the transcontinental railroad, which connected the West and East Coasts of the United States. Many of these workers faced racism and hostility.

a tax specifically applied to Chinese gold miners was levied by the government, followed by a law banning them from mining gold altogether. Additional regulations banned Chinese people from testifying in court—even in their own defense—or from attending public schools. Finally, the Chinese Exclusion Act passed by Congress in 1882 banned almost all Chinese immigration to the United States.

Chinese and other Asian immigrants in the United States were also subject to racist and even violent treatment. Just one of many examples is an 1885 dispute among White and Chinese miners that turned deadly in Rock Springs, Wyoming. A website by the Wyoming State Historical Society describes what happened after angry White miners refused to forget about the dispute and went on to form a mob that stormed into the part of town that was primarily inhabited by Chinese people. According to the website:

> The mob moved into Chinatown from three directions, pulling some Chinese men from their homes and shooting others as they came into the street. Most fled, dash-

ing through the creek, along the tracks or up the steep bluffs and out into the hills beyond. A few ran straight for the mob and met their deaths. White women took part in the killing, too. The mob turned back through Chinatown, looting the shacks and houses, and then setting them on fire. More Chinese were driven out of hiding by the flames and were killed in the streets. Others burned to death in their cellars. Still others died that night out on the hills and prairies from thirst, the cold and their wounds.[8]

In total, twenty-eight Chinese people were killed, fifteen were wounded, and seventy-nine houses were looted and burned. No charges were ever filed against any of the White miners. As a result of immigration restrictions and violence such as this, Chinese immigrants largely stopped coming to the United States for many years.

Other Early Immigrants

However, the United States still needed laborers, so people came in large numbers from other Asian countries, including Japan, Korea, India, and the Philippines. Many of these immigrants were men, but there were also some women and families. While the experiences of immigrants varied widely, overall, each ethnic group faced treatment similar to that of the Chinese: success, followed by racism and exclusion. This was the experience of many of those who arrived from Japan, the next Asian nation after China to send a large number of immigrants to the United States. Most Japanese immigrants started out as laborers, but many ended up owning their own farms. Lee talks about how Japanese farmers quickly became very successful in the western United States. She says, "In 1900, there were thirty-seven Japanese farms in the United States with a combined acreage of 6,474 acres. By 1910, Japanese had 1,816 farms with a total acreage of 99,254. On the eve of World War II, they grew 90 percent of California's snap peas, 67 percent of the state's tomatoes, and 44 percent of its onions."[9]

Like Chinese immigrants had before them, Japanese immigrants soon faced hostility, violent treatment, and legal restrictions such as laws that took away their right to own land or to become citizens. In his 1924 testimony in support of restricting Japanese immigration, V.S. McClatchy, publisher of the *Sacramento Bee* newspaper, gave an opinion that many other Americans agreed with at that time. He said, "Of all races ineligible to citizenship, the Japanese are the least assimilable and the most dangerous to his country." He explained his belief that Japanese immigrants would never assimilate in the United States, saying, "They do not come to this country with any desire or intent to lose their racial or national identities. They come here specifically and professedly for the purpose of colonizing and establishing here permanently the proud Yamato race. They never cease to be Japanese."[10]

All of the anti-Asian sentiment culminated with the Immigration Act of 1924, which stopped immigration from most Asian countries. Under the new law, any foreigner who was ineligible for citizenship because of his or her race or nationality was not allowed to enter the United States. Since Asians had been prohibited from becoming citizens of the United States under previous laws, this meant that they were now prohibited from even immigrating to the United States.

> "In 1900, there were thirty-seven Japanese farms in the United States with a combined acreage of 6,474 acres. By 1910, Japanese had 1,816 farms with a total acreage of 99,254."[9]
>
> —Erika Lee, the granddaughter of Chinese immigrants

The Immigration and Naturalization Act of 1965

It was not until 1965 that Asians were able to immigrate to the United States again in significant numbers. Under the Immigration and Naturalization Act of 1965, immigration policy changed dramatically; criteria for entry into the country were no longer based on race and ethnicity. Instead, under the new regulations, while there would be limits on overall immigration, immigrants would now be admitted based on their skills and their family relationships with US citizens and permanent residents. The History, Art & Archives website of the US House of Representatives summarizes the law, explaining, "Congress erected a legal framework that prioritized highly skilled immigrants and opened the door for people with family already living in the United States. The popular bill passed the House, 318 to 95."[11] Following passage of the new immigration law, a large number of people from many Asian nations began coming to the United States. The Center for Immigration Studies reports that from 1901 to 1920, only 4 percent of immigrants were from Asia, while from 1980 to 1993—after the enactment of new immigration laws—that changed to 39 percent.

Koreans were one group of people who immigrated to the United States in large numbers after the 1965 immigration act. The Migration Policy Institute finds that Korean immigration went from only 11,000 people in 1906 to 290,000 in 1980. While early Korean

President Lyndon B. Johnson signs the Immigration Act of 1965. The legislation led to people from many Asian countries immigrating to the United States, which they had been previously prohibited from doing.

immigrants had been mainly laborers, this new wave of immigrants also included many highly educated professionals. The new Korean immigrants also had a reputation for entrepreneurship. One reason so many Korean immigrants opened their own businesses was that many had trouble finding work because of discrimination and language and cultural differences. BBC journalist Katie Beck talked to some Korean American entrepreneurs in New York City. She tells the story of Sunhee and SeoJun Kim, who emigrated from South Korea in 1986. She says, "Like other Koreans in the US, the Kims spoke little English, so they saw going into business for themselves as their best option." The couple opened their own grocery store, working hard to make it succeed. Beck continues, "To encourage business, the Kims opened their shop 24 hours a day, seven days a week. The couple worked incredibly long hours, driving out to the Hunts Point market before dawn, filling their truck with fruits and vegetables to stock their shelves."[12] As a result of their hard work, their son, Ron, was able to get an education in the United States and later go into politics in New York.

Refugees

In addition to immigrants like the Kims seeking economic opportunity, beginning in 1975 the United States also started to accept a large number of refugees from Southeast Asia. These refugees were escaping war and persecution in their home countries. For example, under the brutal Cambodian Khmer Rouge dictatorship of 1975 to 1979, more than 1 million people died as a result of starvation, overwork, or execution, and many thousands more fled the country to escape a similar fate. Refugees also left Vietnam and Laos, hoping to escape the violence and persecution that resulted when the United States withdrew from the Vietnam War and Communist troops gained control of Vietnam in 1975. The United Nations High Commissioner for Refugees (UNHCR) estimates that overall, from 1975 to 1995 more than 3 million people fled Southeast Asia to escape violence and persecution. It is estimated that the United States accepted more than 1 million of those refugees.

The First Chinese Woman in the United States

Afong Moy is believed to have been one of the first Chinese women to come to the United States. She arrived in 1834 with merchant brothers, who also brought many Chinese goods to sell to Americans. The brothers set up an exhibit space that they called the *Chinese Saloon*, with Moy as the main attraction. Curious spectators could look at Moy, and while they were there, the merchant brothers tried to sell them their merchandise. Moy was just a teenager when she arrived in the United States. Writer Grace Z. Li describes how she entertained audiences, who were fascinated with everything she did, particularly walking on her tiny bound feet. Li says:

> We know that Moy was displayed in a room filled with Chinese furniture so she could sing songs, use chopsticks, and show off her four-inch-long feet, which were small from foot-binding— something Westerners were obsessed with seeing. We know that Moy travelled the East Coast, visiting cities like Boston, Philadelphia, and Washington, D.C., where she met President Andrew Jackson.

> Li calls the exhibit "a human zoo." Moy eventually ended up performing with the P.T. Barnum circus.

Grace Z. Li, "The First Chinese Woman in America Was in a Human Zoo. This Play Tells Her Story," *SF Weekly* (San Francisco), October 18, 2019. www.sfweekly.com.

Many Hmong people were among the Southeast Asian refugees that fled to the United States. The Hmong are an ethnic group that come from China and Southeast Asia. During the Vietnam War, many Hmong soldiers fought with US troops. As a result of that war, more than one hundred thousand Hmong were displaced from their homes in Laos. Because they had fought with the United States, however, tens of thousands were accepted as refugees into the United States. Hmong refugee Cha Fong Lee escaped Laos with his family, living in a refugee camp in Thailand for a year before moving to the United States. He says, "Life in the refugee [camp], that [was] difficult. You cannot go outside, you cannot play around. We had to wait for someone to give us food to eat. That's it." Immigrating to the United States was also stressful. He had no idea what his new home would be like, but it was less risky than remaining in Laos. "We don't know what to do, we don't know where to go," Lee recalls. "We just say, 'OK, come to America.' Then we come here. That's it. We don't know the future."[13]

The United States still accepts a significant number of Asian refugees every year. According to the UNHCR, the majority of them are now from Myanmar, where an ethnic minority group called the Rohingya are denied citizenship and other basic rights by the Myanmar government. The UNHCR says, "More refugees from Myanmar have been resettled in the U.S. in the last decade than from any other country with the exception of the Democratic Republic of the Congo."[14]

"More refugees from Myanmar have been resettled in the U.S. in the last decade than from any other country with the exception of the Democratic Republic of the Congo."[14]

—United Nations High Commissioner for Refugees, the United Nations agency that works to help refugees and other displaced peoples

Hmong people from Laos board a plane to the United States in 1996 after living in refugee camps for the preceding twenty years. Between 1975 and 1995, more than 3 million people fled war and persecution in Southeast Asia.

Japanese Immigrants in Hawaii

While Japanese immigrants on the US mainland faced racism and exclusion, many who immigrated to Hawaii had a better experience. Japanese immigrants started arriving in Hawaii in the mid-1800s. However, unlike on the mainland, immigrants living in Hawaii quickly became an ethnic majority. According to the Library of Congress, indigenous Hawaiians made up 97 percent of Hawaii's population in 1853, but by 1923 that had dropped to only 16 percent, with the biggest percentage of the population being Japanese. The Library of Congress explains that because they were a majority, many Japanese people in Hawaii were not shunned in the same way as those living elsewhere. It says, "By the 1930s, Japanese immigrants, their children, and grandchildren had set down deep roots in Hawaii, and inhabited communities that were much older and more firmly established than those of their compatriots on the mainland. . . . Japanese Hawaiians . . . lived in a multiethnic society in which they played a majority role." For instance, during World War II, most mainland Japanese were forced into internment camps, but most Hawaiian Japanese were not because it would have been impractical to incarcerate such a large percentage of Hawaii's population.

Library of Congress, "Hawaii: Life in a Plantation Society." www.loc.gov.

Recent Immigration

Refugees and many other people continue to immigrate to the United States from all over Asia, for a wide variety of reasons. According to the Migration Policy Institute, in 2019 the largest number of Asian immigrants to the United States came from India, followed by China and then the Philippines. In 2021 the Cato Institute questioned Asian immigrants about their reasons for immigrating to the United States. It found that the main reason was economic opportunity, followed by freedom, a desire to be with family, the need to flee political persecution or violence, and the chance for their children to attend US schools. Just as their reasons for coming to the United States vary widely, so do the experiences of these immigrants. As in the past, many find immediate success in the United States; however, many also encounter racism and restrictions of rights.

CHAPTER TWO

Fighting for Rights

In 1942 more than 120,000 Japanese Americans were living on the US mainland. About two-thirds of them were American citizens who had been born and raised there. However, because of the fact that the United States was at war with Japan, all of these Japanese Americans were suspected of being disloyal to the United States. Almost every one of them was forced to sell, or simply leave behind, their homes, pets, businesses, and most of their property and travel to internment camps sometimes hundreds of miles away. Mary Tsukamoto was one of those interned. She talks about arriving at the camps, saying:

> We saw all these people behind the fence, looking out, hanging onto the wire, and looking out because they were anxious to know who was coming in. But I will never forget the shocking feeling that human beings were behind this fence like animals [crying]. And we were going to also lose our freedom and walk inside of that gate and find ourselves . . . cooped up there . . . when the gates were shut, we knew that we had lost something that was very precious; that we were no longer free.[15]

The United States was also at war with Germany and Italy, but German and Italian Americans were not forced into internment camps. Despite continually protesting that they were loyal Americans, most Japanese Americans were forced to live in the camps until the war ended in 1945. Later, many campaigned for redress, but it was not until 1988 that the US government formally apologized for the internment and offered monetary reparations to those who had been incarcerated. This shocking mistreatment is only one example of how Asian Americans have frequently had to fight to get the same rights as other people living in the United States.

US Citizenship

Citizenship is one of those rights. While early immigrants from many other countries—including Germany, Ireland, and England—were able to become US citizens, it took Asian immigrants more than one hundred years to secure that same right. The reason for this can be found in the attitudes held by many Americans in the 1800s—that Asians were inferior and thus not worthy of citizenship. Madeline Hsu, a professor of history and Asian American studies at the University of Texas at Austin, explains that Asians were viewed as "biologically different and therefore inferior, bearing different culture and civilization, and unassimilable into the United States."[16] The Naturalization Act of 1790, which laid out the rules for US citizenship, stated that only a "free white person"[17] could become a US citizen. This meant that Asians were not eligible for citizenship because they were not White.

Asian immigrants challenged the ban on citizenship numerous times, but courts consistently ruled against them. For instance, in a 1922 Supreme Court case, Japanese immigrant Takao Ozawa argued that after living in the United States for twenty years and meeting all of the requirements for US citizenship, he should be able to become a citizen. He insisted that his skin was as pale as that of White Americans, so he should

"[In the 1800s Asian Americans were seen as] biologically different and therefore inferior, bearing different culture and civilization, and unassimilable into the United States."[16]

—Eiichi Sakauye, a Japanese man

In the wake of the 1941 Japanese attack on Pearl Harbor in Hawaii, thousands of Japanese Americans were forced from their homes to what were known as relocation centers. About two-thirds of these people had been born and raised in the United States.

be categorized as "White" and thus allowed citizenship. The Supreme Court disagreed, finding that "White" meant "persons of the Caucasian Race,"[18] not Asians.

In 1923 the court issued another decision reaffirming that Asians could not become citizens. In that case Bhagat Singh Thind, an immigrant from India, had his naturalization application denied on the grounds that he was not White. He argued that he was a high-caste Hindu, born in a northwestern area of India, and was, "classified by certain scientific authorities as of the Caucasian or Aryan race."[19] As a result, he insisted that according to the 1922 court decision, being part of the Caucasian race meant that he was White and thus eligible for citizenship. The court disagreed, ruling that it was not interested in the scientific definition of *Caucasian*. Instead, it said that *Caucasian* should be defined as it was popularly understood by the average person, in which case it did not include Indians. It was not until 1952 that a new law was passed that abolished racial restrictions on citizenship, and Asian American immigrants were finally able to become US citizens.

Prior to 1952 Asian Americans did have one victory in relation to citizenship. The Supreme Court affirmed their right to birthright citizenship. Birthright citizenship means that a person who is born in the United States is automatically a US citizen, regardless of race or ethnicity. The right to birthright citizenship is established under the Fourteenth Amendment to the US Constitution, which states, "All persons born or naturalized in the United States, and subject to the jurisdiction thereof, are citizens of the United States and of the state wherein they reside. No state shall make or enforce any law which shall abridge the privileges or immunities of citizens of the United States." The court case affirming that right occurred as a result of the experience of Wong Kim Ark, who was born in 1873 to Chinese parents in San Francisco but was not allowed to reenter the United States after an 1895 visit to China. Immigration authorities maintained that because he was Chinese, he was not eligible for US citizenship. Wong contended that since he had been born in the United States, he was automatically a citizen under the Fourteenth Amendment. His case went to the Supreme Court, which ruled in his favor in 1898. This was an important victory for Asian Americans because it gave many the ability to establish permanent legal standing in the United States.

The Right to Own Land

Asian Americans have also had to fight for the right to own land in the United States. In the late 1800s and early 1900s, anti-Asian sentiment was pervasive. It was during this period that a number of western states passed various laws limiting the ability of Asian Americans to own land. Some states even put these laws into their constitutions. For example, Oregon's 1859 constitution stated that no "Chinaman" could own property in that state. Other states prohibited ownership through what were known as alien land laws, meaning laws that prohibited foreigners or noncitizens from owning land. For example, California's Alien Land Law of 1913 stated that aliens who were not eligible for citizenship could not own land. At that time, most Asian Americans were not allowed to become citizens, so this meant that they were also unable to own land. According to the website Densho Encyclopedia, which chronicles

Fighting to Be Recognized

Asian Americans have lived in the United States for hundreds of years and have been an important part of the country's history; however, that role is often not talked about. Chinese American activist Helen Zia comments, "Students can go through their whole educational life, not hearing a single fact or historical reference to Asians in America." Zia and others insist that this needs to change. Actor Daniel Dae Kim testified before Congress in 2021 about discrimination and violence against Asian Americans. He said:

> We must find ways to teach our children the truth about how Asian Americans have contributed to the success of this nation. Let's teach them how many of us helped build the railroad that brought together the east and the west. . . . Let's teach them that the largest mass lynching in our history was of Asian, specifically Chinese, people. . . . Let's also celebrate the fact that the most decorated combat unit in US military history was the 442nd combat team, a unit in World War 2 made up entirely of Asian Americans! These are not moments in Asian American History, this is AMERICAN history. . . . Include our stories. Because they matter.

Quoted in Olivia B. Waxman and Paul Cachero, "11 Moments from Asian American History That You Should Know," *Time*, April 30, 2021. https://time.com.

Daniel Dae Kim, testimony submitted to the US House Committee on the Judiciary Subcommittee on the Constitution, Civil Rights, and Civil Liberties for a Hearing on "Discrimination and Violence Against Asian Americans," March 18, 2021. https://docs.house.gov.

the history of Japanese American exclusion, alien land laws were common. It says, "The total list of states that passed alien land laws or that contained restrictions against aliens ineligible for citizenship owning property in their state constitutions included Arizona, Arkansas, California, Florida, Idaho, Louisiana, Minnesota, Montana, Nebraska, New Mexico, Oregon, Texas, Utah, Washington, and Wyoming."[20]

Asian Americans did not passively accept these new laws, and some figured out ways to get around them. For instance, many Japanese Americans put their farmland in the name of their American-born children, who were citizens and therefore could own land. This is what Japanese American Eiichi Sakauye's family did. He explains, "Gradually, my dad got bigger and bigger in farming. And the alien land law came in effect, so that stopped a person of Japanese ancestry [from being able] to purchase land or, or even to get American citizenship, because they were ineligible to become American citizen[s]. So that put the kink in our expansion." However, Sakauye says that he was born in the United States, and therefore a citizen—which meant he could put the land in his name. The family did this when he turned twenty-one. "Then we started over again increasing our business, because I could do things legally," Sakauye explains. "Heretofore, we couldn't do it legally, because I was underage and also my folks were ineligible to become American citizens."[21] It was not until 1953 that the Supreme Court ruled that alien land laws were unconstitutional.

> "Gradually, my dad got bigger and bigger in farming. And the alien land law came in effect, so that stopped a person of Japanese ancestry unable to purchase land or, or even to get American citizenship."[21]
>
> —Erika Lee, the granddaughter of Chinese immigrants

Farmworker Rights

While some early immigrants owned their own land or businesses, many worked as laborers. However, laborers had to fight for rights too. This was particularly true for farmworkers. Early migrant farmworkers did work that was extremely physically demanding, were paid very little for it, and were poorly treated by their employers and others in the communities where they lived. According to the Equal Justice Initiative, "Migrant workers lacked educational opportunities for their children, lived in poverty and terrible housing conditions, and faced discrimination and violence when they sought fair treatment."[22] The organization explains that any attempts to create workers unions in order to address these problems were violently suppressed.

Filipino farm laborers refused to accept this situation. Instead, they demanded better treatment, persevering with that demand until employers were finally forced to listen to them and make changes. During the 1900s, thousands of Filipino farmworkers came to work in the western United States, and like other farmworkers, many were poorly treated. Although their attempts to change the situation were met with punishment and violence, they did not give up. Filipino immigrant Larry Itliong and others formed the Filipino Agricultural Workers Organizing Committee (AWOC). In 1965 AWOC organized the Delano, California, grape strike, in which workers demanded better pay and working conditions. Filipinos were not the only immigrants who wanted better working conditions, and the National Farm Workers Association—made up of mainly Mexican laborers and led by Cesar Chavez and Dolores Huerta—joined the strike. The two groups eventually merged into the United Farm Workers (UFW). The strikers did not immediately succeed, but eventually the growers were forced to give in to their demands. "The strike would last five years and end in 1970 when the UFW reached collective bargaining agreements with several grape growers, improving the lives of over 10,000 workers,"[23] says Dennis Arguelles of the Asian Pacific Policy and Planning Council, a coalition that advocates for the rights of Asian and Pacific Islander communities in the United States. The 1965

Migrant farmworkers pause to pray during a march that was part of the Delano grape strike of 1965. Filipino immigrants demanding better working conditions organized the strike, which was eventually joined by Mexican laborers as well.

Asian Americans in Government

In 2021 Kamala Harris made history when she registered three important firsts: first female US vice president, first Black vice president, and first vice president of South Asian descent. (Her father is from Jamaica; her mother is from India.)

Despite Harris's trajectory from San Francisco district attorney to California attorney general to US senator from California to US vice president, Harris remains something of an outlier. Asian Americans remain greatly underrepresented in government leadership positions. According to a 2021 report by the Reflective Democracy Campaign, Asian Americans and Pacific Islanders make up 6.1 percent of the US population, but only 0.9 percent of elected leaders in the United States are Asian American or Pacific Islander. William Tong, the first Asian American to be elected as Connecticut attorney general, says, "People still have a hard time seeing and conceiving Asian Americans and Pacific Islanders as good elected officials." Tong and others insist that this needs to change. He says, "There are many more members of Congress than when I was a kid. We have the first AAPI [Asian American or Pacific Islander] Vice President in the history of our country in Kamala Harris but still our voice is not sufficient and in many ways Asian Americans are still invisible in our public life."

Quoted in Nicole Chavez and Priya Krishnakumar, "We Speak About Asian Americans as a Single Block. Here's How Incredibly Complex They Are," CNN, May 1, 2022. www.cnn.com.

strike was important not only because it improved conditions for the workers involved but also because it empowered and inspired people all across the United States to stand up for their rights.

Civil Rights

Another turning point in the Asian American fight for rights was the 1982 murder of Vincent Chin. At that time, there were already many examples of little or no punishment for perpetrators of crimes against Asian Americans. However, Chin's murder represented a breaking point for the Asian American community. In 1982 Americans had been buying more Japanese cars, and the American automobile industry was in decline as a result. Chin—who was Chinese American—was beaten to death by a White autoworker and his stepson who were unhappy with this decline and mistook him for Japanese. His killers received a minimal sentence: each

Marchers protest the light sentences given to the killers of Vincent Chin, a Chinese American who was murdered in a 1982 hate crime. The event prompted outraged Asian Americans from many groups to join forces and demand better treatment from American society.

was fined $3,000 and freed on probation. Explaining his decision, the judge said, "We're talking here about a man who's held down a responsible job with the same company for 17 or 18 years, and his son who is employed and is a part-time student. These men are not going to go out and harm somebody else. I just didn't think that putting them in prison would do any good for them or for society."[24] Asian Americans were outraged. They argued that the men would have received a much more severe punishment if the victim had been White.

The Chin murder was a turning point because it inspired many Asian Americans to work together in a way they never had before to protest unjust treatment and to demand that America do better. Pulitzer Prize–winning journalist and Filipino American Alex Tizon says, "The story became a thread that joined Asian American groups with little previous contact. Help was offered, partnerships were formed, and compacts made among Chinese, Japanese, Taiwanese, Koreans, and Filipinos. . . . A new pan-Asian awareness seemed to come into being."[25] As a result of that new pan-Asian awareness, there has gradually been more public discussion about Asian American civil rights. However, the Asian American community continues to fight for fair treatment.

As all of these stories show, the fight for rights is ongoing. Throughout US history, Asian Americans have been forced again and again to fight for recognition and for fair treatment in the United States.

CHAPTER THREE

Creating New Communities

Anna Regina Gotuaco is Filipina American. She grew up in Daly City, California, which she says has the largest population of Filipino people outside of the Philippines. Later she moved to New York City. Gotuaco says that she sometimes feels homesick for her Filipino culture. One thing that makes her feel better is visiting Little Manila, an area in Queens with a heavy concentration of Filipino shops, restaurants, and people. She talks about the first time she visited Little Manila, saying:

> Walking through Little Manila gave me the odd sensation of being home. I walked down Roosevelt Avenue, rain falling hard as if I was truly in the Philippines, a sense of déjà vu overtaking me. Middle-aged people lounged on the sidewalk, sitting on a chair next to a large blue cooler, selling popular Filipino street foods like *taho*, *balut* and garlic peanuts. The people in Little Manila spoke a language that sounded like home, sold food that my *nanay* [mother] makes and exuded a sense of togetherness. It was a place where Filipino culture was preserved and given the space to thrive.[26]

Little Manila in Queens is just one of numerous Asian ethnic enclaves across the United States. Many Asian cultures have their own versions of Little Manila, including Chinatown, Koreatown, and Little Tokyo. These various enclaves are just one of a variety of different ways that Asian Americans have created strong Asian communities in the United States. At the same time, many maintain strong community relationships with their country of origin.

Ethnic Enclaves

From the beginning, ethnic enclaves like Little Manila have helped connect Asian Americans to one another and to their culture and have provided support for those who need it. These communities—complete with homes, shops, restaurants, churches, and more—often resemble the towns and cities where immigrants or their ancestors once lived. Among the most familiar of these communities are the Chinatowns found in San Francisco, Los Angeles, and New York City. According to the Library of Congress:

> Chinatowns provided Chinese immigrants with the social support networks that were not available to them anywhere else. . . . [Associations in Chinatowns] found jobs for new arrivals, cared for the sick and poor, and arranged for the bones of the dead to be sent back to their homeland. These associations soon became like a secondary system of government, and their leaders served as representatives to the non-Chinese population, sometimes becoming well-known public figures.[27]

For early immigrants in particular, Chinatowns, Japantowns, Koreatowns, and others were often the only places to escape the racism that was widespread and even sanctioned by the government.

Today many ethnic enclaves are popular tourist attractions. However, they continue to fulfill an important role as a place for Asian Americans to relax

"Chinatowns . . . provided Chinese immigrants with the social support networks that were not available to them anywhere else."[27]

—Library of Congress, the national library of the United States

A woman serves Filipino food at a street fair in New York City. The area of Queens, New York, known as Little Manila, boasts a heavy concentration of Filipino shops, restaurants, and people.

and escape the judgments of others. Jeff Yang, who launched one of the first national Asian American magazines, says, "Chinatown. Koreatown. Little Saigon. Little Tokyo. The largest and best-known Asian ethnic enclaves in America tend to be framed as mini theme parks—pocket-sized versions of their counterparts across the Pacific that exist to provide a fun and inexpensive day-trip for non-Asian culture tourists." However, he explains that to Asian Americans, these places are far more than a tourist destination. He says:

> For those who live beyond their borders, they're a spiritual tether to the motherland, a gathering point for families and friends, and a refueling station for supplies and ingredients that just can't be found anywhere else. For those who live within them they're a place of safety from the assimilationist pressure and casual racism of a society where Asians are still a minority in all but a handful of cities and in all but a handful of states.[28]

Asian Pacific American Heritage Month

Every year, during the month of May, the United States celebrates its Asian communities. May is Asian Pacific American Heritage Month, which is a celebration of all Asians and Pacific Islanders who live in the United States. Asian Pacific American Heritage Month was established by Congress in 1979 and was originally only a week long. It was later expanded to include the whole month of May. May was chosen because the first Japanese immigrants to the United States arrived on May 7, 1843, and also because the transcontinental railroad—which would not have been finished without Chinese immigrants—was completed on May 10, 1869. Cynthia Choi, cofounder of the organization Stop AAPI Hate, explains that Asian Pacific American Heritage Month is a time to celebrate all of the special things that Asians and Pacific Islanders bring to the United States. She says, "This is a celebration of our history, of our culture . . . and all the different ways in which our community has really demonstrated that we're not only here to stay, we are a part of this fabric—a part of this country."

Quoted in Rina Torchinsky, "The Story Behind Asian Pacific American Heritage, and Why It's Celebrated in May," NPR, May 2, 2022. www.npr.org.

Community Organizations

Asians have also created strong communities in the United States by establishing many different Asian American organizations, including churches, schools, and sports clubs. These organizations provide a gathering place for people with similar interests, such as religion or sports, but they also connect Asian Americans to other people who share their cultural heritage. Asian American churches, schools, and other organizations teach their members about their culture, provide help when it is needed, and foster a sense of community. For example, the Los Angeles area is home to a large Filipino community. The Filipino Cultural School is one of many Filipino organizations in the city that celebrates and supports the Filipino community. It uses song, dance, and history lessons to educate young people about their heritage and tries to help them understand what it means to be Filipino and encourage them to feel proud of their culture.

Los Angeles also has a large Korean population and many different Korean community organizations. Writer Lisa Kwon, who lives in Koreatown in Los Angeles, writes about the role played by Korean churches in helping Korean immigrants get a start in business. She tells the story of Young Soo Song, a Korean immigrant who wanted to open a plumbing business in Los Angeles. "When he opened shop, he sought advice from his elders at Grace Church," she writes. "He found himself nervously calculating the different factors that go into starting a business but choosing the right name bogged him down the most. Hearing his plight, Song's pastor told him simply to start."[29] Song decided to name his business Grace Plumbing "after the church told me that there's nothing to worry about . . . just lead with faith and start.'"[30] Kwon explains that churches not only offer advice like this, they also help support businesses such as Song's by encouraging other church members to patronize those businesses.

Bigger Communities in Bigger Cities

The existence of strong Asian communities varies across the United States. While Asian Americans live all over the country—in cities and rural areas—overall there tend to be bigger Asian communities in larger cities. For example, New York, Los Angeles, and San Francisco have some of the largest Asian American populations in the United States. The state of Hawaii also has a very large population of Asian Americans. Asian Americans are also more likely to live in the western United States than in other parts of the country. According to the Pew Research Center, 45 percent of Asian Americans live in the West, and almost 30 percent live in California.

Some people say that it is much easier to grow up in large cities or other areas where there are many other Asian Americans, rather than in smaller towns or rural areas where there are very few other Asian Americans. Journalist Karen Turner shares the results of a survey of Asian Americans that reveals this. For instance, one of the people who responded is Korean American Nicole Chung. Chung grew up in a community of mainly White people with no other Korean Americans, and she says that it was

A man bicycles down Grant Avenue, the main thoroughfare in San Francisco's Chinatown. Such communities historically provided familiarity and social support for new immigrants, as well as a haven from society's racism.

hard to live in a place where no one else looked like her. She explains, "Because I didn't see anyone else like me as a little kid, sometimes I really did feel like the only Asian—even though, intellectually, I knew I wasn't."[31]

Like Chung, Japanese American Akemi Johnson grew up in a predominantly White community and found it hard. She says, "I didn't want anything to do with my Japanese American identity." However, when she was in her twenties, Johnson moved to Hawaii, and she felt that life was much easier. She explains, "In Hawaii, being Asian American and being mixed are the norms, and I experienced the privilege, power, and ease that come with that. People could pronounce my name; everywhere, I saw my Japanese American culture reflected back at me; and an Asian-white face like mine was both common and held up as an ideal."[32]

"Because I didn't see anyone else like me as a little kid, sometimes I really did feel like the only Asian—even though, intellectually, I knew I wasn't."[31]

—Nicole Chung, a Korean American woman

One of the survey respondents says that she actually moved to a big city with a large Asian population so that her children would not have the negative experiences that she did. She says, "I moved to the Bay Area to raise my kids so that they don't have to experience the 'othering' in the way that I did."[33]

Transnational Communities

In addition to creating strong communities in the United States, many Asian Americans maintain strong relationships with their country of origin. This is known as transnationalism. Author Erika Lee cites the example of Pratik and Dipa Patel, both of whom immigrated to the United States from India. They both applied for US citizenship five years after arriving. Pratik works for a telecommunications firm and is also getting his master's degree from Boston University. Dipa works at a computer manufacturing firm. Lee says, "Their two young daughters are growing up learning American nursery rhymes, and recently the Patel family bought their own home in the southern New Hampshire suburbs. By all appearances, the Patels are living the American Dream." However, they have not given up their connection to India. Lee explains:

> The Patels are pursuing the Indian Dream as well. Pratik and Dipa regularly send money home to support their retired parents in Gujarat. Pratik donates to the computer school he helped found in his home village, and in addition to paying the mortgage of their home in New Hampshire, they have also renovated their family home in Bodei. . . . Another way that they remain connected to their home state of Gujarat is through religion. They worship every week at the Hindu temple in Lowell, Massachusetts, and belong to ISSO, a Hindu denomination in Gujarat.[34]

While not all Asian Americans live transnationally, researchers are finding that many do. In recent years it has become easier for immigrants to maintain connections with two different countries.

This is because changes in travel have made it cheaper and easier to travel long distances, and technological advancements such as social media have made it easier to keep in contact with people in other countries.

Living transnationally can take many different forms. For example, some people have dual citizenship and spend time living in both countries. Some families send only their children to the United States for schooling. Others leave their children behind and come to the United States for work, sending money home. Lee explains that many Asian Americans also live transnationally through culture and the things they consume:

> Indian immigrants in the Bay Area, for example, frequently visit Indian grocery stores to purchase lentils, spices and other ingredients crucial to Indian cooking. They also buy a variety of other consumer goods imported from India like cosmetics, music, Bollywood films, religious icons, clothes, and jewelry. Purchasing these goods . . . reminds immigrants of home and allows them to remain connected to India.[35]

Businesses like the Indian spice shop pictured here provide immigrant customers with goods that remind them of and allow them to feel connected to their home country.

The Oldest Chinatown in the United States

There are many different Chinatowns in the United States, but the oldest, and one of the largest, is in San Francisco. According to one travel website, "Chinatown's twenty-four blocks are home to approximately 15,000 Chinese residents which makes this the most densely populated neighborhood in all of San Francisco."

San Francisco's Chinatown was founded in the 1800s, when Chinese immigrants started coming to the United States. It was an unofficial port of entry for many of these immigrants, providing them with the help and resources that they needed to begin their lives in the United States. It also provided a haven from the bigotry and restrictive laws that that drove Chinese workers from the gold mines as the US economy weakened.

Chinatown today is a unique and thriving community. The "Chinatown Resource Guide," produced by PBS, describes it as "an American neighborhood, an old neighborhood, an immigrant neighborhood, where the old country still lives inside the new one. The past and the present are inseparably woven together in this neighborhood."

America from the Road, "Chinatown San Francisco: What to See & Where to Eat," December 14, 2019. https://americafromtheroad.com.

PBS, "Chinatown Resource Guide." www.pbs.org.

There is disagreement about the effect of living transnationally. Some people argue that living that way can make it more difficult for Asian Americans, not allowing them to fully become a part of either culture because they are trying to live in two different cultures at the same time. Others contend that as changes in travel and communication make different parts of the world increasingly interconnected, transnational living will become more and more common. Lee says, "In a world increasingly connected through globalization, we're all learning to become global Americans."[36] Asians living in the United States have created many new communities, both transnational and otherwise, and they continue to do so.

CHAPTER FOUR

Embracing Identity

Bee Vue Yang is a first-generation Hmong American, and she is extremely proud of her Hmong heritage. She says, "I am proud of who I am. I am proud of the Hmong language. . . . I have an immense appreciation for anything that resembles being Hmong." However, Yang did not always feel that way. She says that as a child, being Hmong made her life harder in some ways—for instance, her parents did not speak English—and she desperately tried to dissociate from her culture. She says that when she was younger, "I disowned myself and disowned my Hmong identity. I didn't want anything to do with being Hmong."[37] Yang's story echoes those of many Asian Americans who feel pride for their cultures but have found that being Asian American can also mean facing some challenges.

Feeling like Race Does Matter

One of the biggest challenges that Asian Americans say they face in relation to identity is that people often treat them a certain way or assume certain things about them simply because of their race. Taiwanese American Sam You explains that when he was younger, he tried to distance himself from his Taiwanese heritage in an attempt to be treated as an American, not an Asian. However, he says, he soon realized that people would always look at him, see that he is Asian, and treat him a certain way because of that. He says, "I realize that it doesn't matter how I think of myself. . . . It's literally about nothing aside from how we look." Chinese American Geraldine Lim agrees, saying, "As much as I didn't want it to be true, race very much matters in America."[38]

> "As much as I didn't want it to be true, race very much matters in America."[38]
>
> —Geraldine Lim, a Chinese American woman

This focus on race has a significant impact on Asians living in the United States. Law professor and writer Frank H. Wu explains, "It shapes every aspect of my life—and everyone else's."[39] Exactly how life is shaped by being Asian American can vary widely. Some people say that they like their Asian heritage because it makes them feel unique. Others contend that stereotyping exposes them to discrimination.

Of those people who do face discrimination and negative stereotypes—or even just unwanted attention—because they are Asian, some say that they grow up resenting their heritage.

Girls perform a traditional Hmong dance at a festival in Columbus, Ohio. Many immigrants embrace their culture but find it difficult while coping with stereotypes that influence how others perceive them.

That is what happened to professional illustrator Krishna M. Sadasivam. He says that he was born into a traditional Indian household in Canada, in a town where there was a thriving Indian community, and being Asian there never caused him any problems. However, when he was still a child, Sadasivam's family moved to Charlotte, North Carolina, where there were not a lot of Indians. For the first time his race and culture suddenly made him feel very different from everyone else, and he did not feel like he fit in. As a result, he attempted to distance himself from his culture. For example, he says that his mother tried to give him Indian food for his school lunch, but he did not want it because none of the other students had Indian food for lunch. He says, "I didn't need yet another reason to be so obviously different. I might as well have been an alien." Because he hated the way that his Indian identity made him stand out, Sadasivam says, "I grew up resenting my roots."[40]

Some Asian Americans say that they purposely try to cover up their Asian heritage in an attempt to blend in with everyone else. Steven Chu has a German mother and a Chinese father. He says that as a child, he realized that his life would be easier if he tried to hide his Chinese identity. He explains, "I decided if I was going to fit in and make things better for myself, I am going to forget about the Chinese part of myself and be the Caucasian person." Chu says he continued to suppress his Chinese identity into his adulthood because it seemed to make everything easier. "People didn't make fun of me as much," he says, "so throughout school and then in the workplace, I learned to show up more as that Caucasian person. I felt like that was the only way I could be a legitimate sales professional and thrive."[41]

Something to Be Proud Of

However, Chu and many others say that while they may have resented their identity or tried to hide it at some point in their lives, they later came to regret doing so, because they realized that being Asian was an important part of their identity. Korean American

Origin of *Asian American*

The term *Asian American* is believed to have first been used in 1968 by University of California, Berkeley student activists Emma Gee and Yuji Ichioka. Gee and Ichioka were creating a student organization to fight against the oppression of people of Asian descent, and they called it the Asian American Political Alliance. Ichioka explains that uniting different Asian American groups under one name gave them more strength in the fight for equality. He says, "There were so many Asians out there in the political demonstrations but we had no effectiveness. Everyone was lost in the larger rally. We figured that if we rallied behind our own banner, behind an Asian American banner, we would have an effect on the larger public." Adopting the term *Asian American* was also a way to reject other derogatory terms such as *Oriental* that were often used for people of Asian descent.

Quoted in Anna Purna Kambhampaty, "In 1968, These Activists Coined the Term 'Asian American'—and Helped Shape Decades of Advocacy," *Time*, May 22, 2020. https://time.com.

Jason J. Han is a cardiac surgery resident in Philadelphia. When he first arrived in the United States, he changed his name in order to blend in better but later felt regret about doing this. Han says, "On my first day in the United States, a neighbor came up to me and asked my name. As a 10-year-old who had just arrived from Korea and did not speak any English at the time, I replied timidly: 'Ji Seung.' He initially seemed confused. Then a few seconds later he exclaimed as if he had caught an error. 'Oh, your name is Jason! Nice to meet you.'" According to Han, he was so desperate to blend in that he did not correct the neighbor. He continues, "So, less than 24 hours after coming to the United States, I had, without even so much as an objection, let my name be changed to Jason."[42]

Years later Han realized that he had lost an important part of his Korean identity by giving up his Korean name. It took him a long time to find that identity again—and then to embrace it. Ultimately, Han came to realize that being Asian is something to be proud of, and he wants to make sure that other Asian Americans know that too. "I want to be a strong voice for those out there who are looking for their places in this society," says Han. "I want to tell them that fitting in does not mean quietly assimilating. It means being accepted for exactly who we are."[43]

Diana Elizabeth, who calls herself "American Born Chinese," understands this perspective because she has experienced similar feelings over time. She views her Asian identity as something special because it is part of what makes her unique. She notes, "When you're young, you know how that is, you just want to fit and blend in. . . . You don't realize that the older you become the more you want to stand out and not blend in."[44] Being Chinese American makes her stand out, she says, and that is a good thing.

> "Fitting in does not mean quietly assimilating. It means being accepted for exactly who we are."[43]
>
> —Jason J. Han, a Korean American physician

Contributions of Asian Americans

Across the United States, there are millions of Asian Americans, all unique, who have made US culture far richer by deciding to establish their homes there. Vietnamese immigrant Viet Tran explains that immigrants from Asia and other parts of the world make the United States a better and more interesting place to live. He says, "The diversity of our nation is what makes us stronger and more connected, and immigrants are a part of the beautiful fabric of this country. Throughout history, immigrants have enriched the foundation and culture of the U.S. with our resilient narratives, colorful traditions and innovative contributions."[45]

One specific way that Asian Americans have enriched the United States is through the numerous technological advances they have pioneered. For example, most Americans have used the popular video-sharing site YouTube. That site was created in 2005 by Bangladeshi German American Jawed Karim and Taiwanese American Steven Chen, in addition to Chad Hurley, a native of Pennsylvania. Email is also an important part of life for most people. In 1996 Indian American Sabeer Bhatia cofounded the email service Hotmail, which turned into Microsoft Outlook, one of

Asian Americans have made many important contributions to American society. Bangladeshi-German American Jawed Karim (right) and Taiwanese American Steven Chen (left), along with Pennsylvania native Chad Hurley (center), created the popular website YouTube.

the most popular email servers in the world. Another technological advance that came from an Asian American is the USB, a common way to transfer data from one device to another. It was invented in the 1990s by Indian American computer architect Ajay Bhatt.

Fashion and architecture in the United States have also been greatly impacted by Asian Americans. Well-known Asian American architects include Japanese American Minoru Yamasaki, who designed the original World Trade Center, and Chinese American I.M. Pei, who designed the John F. Kennedy Presidential Library and Museum and the Rock & Roll Hall of Fame and Museum. Another well-known Asian American architect is Chinese American Maya Lin. As a twenty-one-year-old undergraduate student, Lin beat out more than fourteen hundred competitors with her winning design for the Vietnam Veterans Memorial in Washington,

"The diversity of our nation is what makes us stronger and more connected, and immigrants are a part of the beautiful fabric of this country."[45]

—Viet Tran, a Vietnamese immigrant

Making Laws That Help Protect Victims of Sexual Assault

Vietnamese American Amanda Nguyen has made life better for thousands of people in the United States by advocating for the rights of survivors of sexual assault. After becoming the victim of sexual assault herself, Nguyen discovered how many challenges were faced by other survivors. For example, her rape kit would be destroyed within six months unless she petitioned otherwise. She founded Rise, an organization that helps other survivors of sexual assault, and also wrote the 2016 Sexual Assault Survivors' Rights Act, which gives victims access to a free medical examination and lets their rape kits be saved for twenty years. Nguyen says that her parents raised her to believe that she would sometimes have to fight for her freedom. In the case of rights for sexual assault survivors, she says, "I realized I could accept injustice, or I could rewrite the law." Nguyen was nominated for the 2019 Nobel Peace Prize for her work.

Quoted in Sara Gaynes Levy, "Meet the Woman Who Changed the Law to Protect Survivors of Sexual Assault," Shondaland, March 21, 2019. www.shondaland.com.

DC. In the fashion industry, Anna Sui, Vera Wang, Kimora Lee Simmons, Jason Wu, and Alexander Wang are just a few of the famous Asian American designers who have helped shape the industry. "From high fashion to street style, Asian-American designers have been a huge influence on a global scale for decades,"[46] says writer Sammi Wong.

Asian Americans have also introduced Americans to a wide variety of different foods, many of which have become extremely popular. *New York Times* writer Ligaya Mishan lists just a few of the many ingredients that originated in various Asian countries but have become popular in kitchens and restaurants across the United States. She says:

The briny rush of soy [sauce]; ginger's low burn; pickled cabbage with that heady funk so close to rot. Vinegar applied to everything. Fish sauce like the underbelly of the sea. Palm sugar, velvet to cane sugar's silk. Coconut milk slowing the tongue. Smoky black cardamom with its menthol aftermath. Sichuan peppercorns that paralyze the lips and turn speech to a burr, and Thai bird chilies that immolate everything they touch. Fat rice grains that cling, that you can scoop up with your hands.[47]

These once exotic ingredients have become so popular in the United States that they have actually come to be seen by some people as American ingredients.

A Complicated Identity

The United States has undoubtedly benefited from all the contributions that Asian Americans have made. Yet many Asians living in the United States stress that for them, having a connection to multiple cultures remains complicated. They explain that this is because it sometimes feels like they do not fully belong in either culture. As Vishakha N. Desai, former president of the Asia Society, states, "Too often Asian Americans end up trapped in an unwelcome binary: claimed by neither Asia nor America, and belonging nowhere."[48]

Some Asian Americans identify neither as fully Asian nor fully American, instead characterizing themselves as a pairing of both cultures that is its own unique identity.

CNN journalist Selina Wang talks about feeling like this on a visit to China. She tells her story:

Last summer, a Chinese man approached me on a crowded Beijing street and asked me in Mandarin if I was Chinese American. It seemed innocent enough, as I was speaking English with expat friends. But after I nodded, he switched to English and bellowed "go back to where you f**king came from." These stinging words are familiar for Asian Americans living in the United States. But it was jarring to hear the phrase shouted at me in China. In the moment, I let out a laugh: As a Chinese American, I have now been told to get out of each country for the other.[49]

At that moment, Wang adds, she realized that as a Chinese American, she will always be a foreigner, whether she is in China or the United States.

Some Asian Americans look at their dual cultures in a slightly different way, characterizing themselves as neither Asian nor American but instead as a pairing of both Asian and American cultures to form a unique identity. Asian American student M.K. explains, "To me, being an Asian American means you identify with a unique culture that can't be defined by Asian culture or American culture. And the older I've gotten, the more I've realized that it's not really a combination of the two either, it is its own entity." M.K. finds this unique identity rewarding, saying, "Being an Asian American means you can identify and find common experiences with an incredibly diverse community whether you're first generation or fourth generation, Korean American or Indian American."[50]

However, that identity is not without challenges. As Asian American student A.P. adds, "Being Asian American is being Asian and American, two separate and often clashing worlds. Navigating that clash is the hardest part."[51] Asian Americans throughout the United States navigate that clash every day. Many feel proud of their identity, but many also face challenges as a result of it.

CHAPTER FIVE

Ongoing Challenges

Yong Ae Yue was a sixty-three-year-old Korean American who lived near Atlanta, Georgia. She was a mother to two sons—Elliott and Robert Peterson—and a grandmother to eight children. Her sons say that she loved her children and grandchildren and taught them to work hard and to embrace their Korean heritage. She also enjoyed her job at the Aromatherapy Spa. On March 16, 2021, Yue was at work when a gunman walked into the spa and shot and killed her. He killed a total of eight people in three Atlanta-area spas that day. Six of them were Asian women. Most people see this as a hate crime and argue that it is just one example of the ways that Asian Americans continue to be targeted based on their race. Asians living in the United States are continually forced to confront negative stereotypes, discrimination, and hate based on their Asian identity.

Recent Increase in Discrimination and Hate

The COVID-19 pandemic brought with it an increase in public displays of discrimination and violence against Asian Americans. The organization Stop AAPI Hate tracks hate crimes against Asian Americans, and it reports that from March 2020 to December 2021, there were 10,905 reports of hate incidents against Asian Americans and Pacific Islanders. Of those reports, the majority (63 percent) were verbal harassment, but a significant percentage (16.2 percent) were physical assaults. The Center for the Study of Hate & Extremism also tracks hate crimes against Asian Americans. In the first quarter of 2021, it reported that compared to the previous year, hate crimes reported to the police in sixteen of the largest US cities and counties had risen by 164 percent. The Pew Research Center found a recent increase in hate crimes against Asian Americans as well. In 2021 it reported that almost a third of Asian American adults felt afraid that someone might threaten them or physically attack them.

In addition to all of these statistics, there are personal stories from all over the United States showing just how many Asians have experienced hate crimes since the pandemic began. For instance, in 2021 photographer Eric Lee talked to Asian American teenagers in New York City and found that many had been targets of hate or were afraid that they would be. Some of the teens said they no longer do certain things like walk alone, because they are afraid of being confronted or attacked. For instance, seventeen-year-old Vicki Z. told him that she was walking home with her friends one day when a man walked up to her and said, "Corona-free NYC!"[52] Now when she walks alone, she wears a cap to cover her face and headphones to block out comments from people. Nineteen-year-old Emma Tang told Lee that she was sitting at a table with her friends when a man hit her over the head with a dirty sheet. She still thinks about how something worse could have happened to her.

Not Something New

Researchers suggest a number of reasons for the increasing expressions of hate that have come with the pandemic. One is the fact that the virus is thought to have originated in China. Some Americans have turned this into a vendetta against anyone of Asian descent. Another reason is the need to blame someone for the increased stress and difficulties brought about by the pandemic. For some people, Asian Americans have been a convenient target for scapegoating. Finally, during the first two critical years of the pandemic, the US president at the time, Donald Trump, made numerous racist, anti-Asian comments in public. His comments, including descriptions of COVID-19 as "Chinese flu" and "kung flu,"[53] likely encouraged hate and discrimination against Asian Americans. "Academic studies substantiate the notion that government speech and actions towards racial minority groups can influence the level of hate crimes committed against those groups,"[54] says Shirin Sinnar, professor of law at Stanford Law School.

> "Government speech and actions towards racial minority groups can influence the level of hate crimes committed against those groups."[54]
>
> —Shirin Sinnar, a professor of law at Stanford Law School

While the recent increase in hate crimes is alarming, many experts point out that hate directed at Asian Americans is not new. Asian Americans have experienced hate throughout US history; it has simply become more severe—and thus more noticeable—during the pandemic. Jeff Yang, Phil Yu, and Philip Wang are the authors of *Rise: A Pop History of Asian America from the Nineties to Now*. They write, "Asian Americans will tell you that this hate and hostility directed toward our community are not new sentiments—they've just been given the green light to be out in the open, unchecked."[55]

The 2020 COVID-19 pandemic, which originated in China, sparked a significant increase in anti-Asian violence and discrimination. Here, participants protest such violence at a San Francisco rally held in March 2021.

Negative Stereotypes

Hatred is not the only type of negative treatment that Asian Americans experience because of their race. Most Asian Americans, including those born in the United States, have endured questions from strangers about their origins. At times the questioners seem incapable of understanding that an Asian American could actually be from America. Journalist and author Helen Zia recounts some of these types of exchanges:

> There is a drill that nearly all Asians in America have experienced more times than they can count. Total strangers will interrupt with the absurdly existential question "What are you?" Or the equally common inquiry "Where are you from?" . . . . My standard reply to "What are you?" is "American," and to "Where are you from?" "New Jersey." These, in my experience, cause great displeasure. Eyebrows arch as the questioner tries again. "No, where are you really from?"[56]

People also tend to make assumptions about someone who looks Asian. Diana Elizabeth says that people often assume that she speaks Chinese and is experienced in Chinese cooking techniques because she looks Chinese. She has trouble understanding this way of thinking. "If you live and grow up in America and that's where you live your life, that's just not reasonable. Europeans came to the US hundreds of years ago and no one is doing the same things as their French or English ancestors with proper tea time, or speak[ing] French or German."[57]

Asian Americans are often stereotyped in other ways too. One common stereotype is that Asians are always submissive and agreeable. Sara Ahmed is a writer who was born in Pakistan and lives in the United States. She often feels like her clients assume she will be passive because of her race. She explains, "It always felt like there was this huge stereotype that I was constantly tackling [that] perhaps I'll be very subservient and a little more meek about speaking up."[58] Another common stereotype is that

First-Generation Immigrants Are More Likely to Ignore Discrimination

Anti-Asian hate and discrimination can be directed at anyone, whether they have recently immigrated to the United States or were born and raised there. However, the response appears to differ by generation. Researchers have found that in some cases, first-generation immigrants seem to be more likely to ignore racist treatment. Many are also unaware of how common it is. *Los Angeles Times* journalist Jeong Park explains that one reason for this is that first-generation immigrants are often focused on other things. He says, "First-generation Asian immigrants . . . are often focused on building a stable life in their adopted country. Some experienced war in their homelands, so a few ugly words or even a physical assault seem insignificant compared with what they have seen." In contrast, later generations of immigrants are often much more likely to notice racism. He writes, "Their children and grandchildren, born in the U.S., are more likely to feel completely American and not tolerate any insinuation that they are foreigners."

Jeong Park, "Asian Americans Are Having 'The Talk' About Racism for the First Time—with Their Parents," *Los Angeles Times*, April 5, 2022. www.latimes.com.

all Asians are smart. Amber Ly is a Cambodian American teen growing up in San Francisco. "When I'm at school, my teachers and peers still treat me like I'm supposed to be some kind of genius," she says, "I've spent the last four years in high school, feeling ashamed because I'm a B student."[59] Fifteen-year-old Rhea Park has found that this stereotype prevents her from getting the help she needs in school. "The teachers, whenever I needed help like, they're like 'Oh, it's okay. You can figure it out,'"[60] she says. Yet another common stereotype is of Asian men as not very athletic or good looking. For instance, Bernard Bach, a Tennessee-born New Yorker of Vietnamese descent, comments, "One of the worst things I hear is, 'You're good-looking for an Asian.'"[61] While none of these stereotypes is true, Asian Americans complain that it is very common to encounter them.

People react to this stereotyping in different ways. Some Asian Americans report that they find it easier to quietly accept stereotyping and not cause trouble. Journalist Mallika Kallingal spoke to people who had faced racism as a result of being Asian American. Kallingal relates the views of seventeen-year-old Tiffany Pham about why some people quietly accept negative stereotyping: "Tiffany . . . says sometimes when Asian Americans face discrimination, they've been 'conditioned to just sit passively and endure it, rather than sticking up for ourselves or fighting back.' . . . She says a lot of Asian American children are conditioned to think that humiliating jokes and comments are something that happens and 'not worth discussing.'"[62]

However, many Asian Americans refuse to accept those stereotypes and humiliating comments. Tina Chen Craig, founder of U Beauty and Bag Snob, does not accept the labels that others have tried to force on her. Instead of being quiet and submissive like a stereotypical Asian girl, she says, "I was loud and demand-

> "We are not the 'quiet minority' that will be passively silenced and continuously stereotyped."[63]
>
> —Tina Chen Craig, founder of U Beauty and Bag Snob

A common stereotype about Asian Americans is that they are all highly intelligent. This can lead to enormous pressure on young students to perform well academically.

Viewing Asian Women as Sex Objects

Americans often view Asian American women as sex objects. Liann Kaye, who lives in New York City, describes an encounter with a man who refused to accept that she was not interested in him. She was walking down the street, trying not to attract attention, when the man approached her and said, "Ni hao, beautiful." (*Ni hao* is the Mandarin Chinese word for "hello.")

The first thought that entered Kaye's mind was: "Go away. Go away. Go away." But the man did not give up. He pursued her, shouting "Hey! I said, 'Ni hao!'" When she did not respond, he became more insistent: "Hello! I'm talking to you!"

And then he grabbed her arm. She feared he might bruise it or break it. "Where are you from, sexy?" he asked, as though he had a right to an answer. Kaye told him to stop, to go away. She noticed he seemed startled by her American accent. "What?" he responded. "You don't want a compliment? C'mon, I thought you and I might get a *happy ending*."

Kaye says this type of encounter happens every day to Asian women walking down public streets in New York City.

Liann Kaye, "As an Asian Woman, I Know Firsthand That Sexism and Racism Are Inextricably Linked," Global Citizen, March 19, 2021. www.globalcitizen.org.

---

ed attention. I spent a lot of time in detention. I recall a few teachers (usually white males) commenting that I wasn't very 'Oriental' because of my boisterous behavior. They wanted me to know my place." Craig insists, "We are not the 'quiet minority' that will be passively silenced and continuously stereotyped."[63]

The "Model Minority" Myth

Another challenge for Asian Americans is having to confront the "model minority" stereotype. The USC Pacific Asia Museum defines this term this way: "Asian Americans are often stereotyped as studious, successful, smart—a model minority who excel in education and accomplish the 'American Dream.'"[64]

Even though this might seem like a positive stereotype, critics argue that it is harmful in many ways. One major problem is that the model minority stereotype hides the fact that a significant number of Asians in the United States are not actually living the American Dream. Those people get overlooked, critics say, and do not get the help they need because of the mistaken belief that all Asian Americans are doing well. "Highlighting only the successful characteristics obscures the significant proportion of Asian Americans who still struggle to survive, live in poverty, are unemployed or underemployed,"[65] says Erika Lee.

According to the Pew Research Center, while Asian Americans as a whole do have a higher average income than other Americans, there are also a significant number of Asian Americans who live in poverty. For example, the center reports that Burmese Americans (a reference to people whose families have come from the country of Burma, now called Myanmar) have an average income of only $44,400, which is lower than the US average of $61,800 and far below the Asian American average of $85,800. It also says that about 25 percent of Americans of Mon-

Despite stereotypes that suggest Asian Americans are all very much alike, in reality there is a wide diversity in their experiences. However, one thing that they have in common is that they have both transformed, and been transformed by, life in the United States.

golian descent live in poverty, compared to only about 10 percent of Asian Americans as a whole and 13 percent of other Americans. The needs of these groups are often overlooked because of the mistaken belief that all Asian Americans are well off.

Journalist Li Zhou writes about Cambodian refugee Sarath Suong. Suong's family came to the United States along with thousands of other refugees who were fleeing Cambodia's brutal Khmer Rouge regime. After settling in the Boston area, the Suong family struggled. Suong says that many Americans did not understand where he had come from, or treated him differently because of the color of his skin, and he often felt unwelcome. Suong always wondered why his experience was so different from that of other Asian Americans. "Growing up for me, I felt so disempowered. . . . I was always wondering why people in my community were getting harassed and being thrown in jail by the police."[66] Suong's experience did not seem to match depictions of the lives of other Asian Americans. "As white writers pushed the idea of the 'model minority myth' . . . Suong feared for his friends' deportations and violence at the hands of cops,"[67] Zhou writes. Suong's story is echoed across the United States by other Asian Americans who have difficulty coming to terms with the fact that their lives are not the same as what is portrayed by the model minority stereotype.

Overall, there is huge diversity in the experiences of Asian Americans. However, one thing that they have in common is that they have both transformed life in the United States and been transformed by it. Lee says, "One thread that connects this history across time is how Asian Americans have—over successive generations—continued to build communities and shape American life in ways that have been central to the making of the United States today."[68]

SOURCE NOTES

Introduction: A Diverse Group of People

1. Karen Turner, "The Many Asian Americas," *Vox*, May 12, 2021. www.vox.com.
2. US Census Bureau, "About the Topic of Race," March 1, 2022. www.census.gov.
3. *Teen Vogue* Staff and Jonathan Frydman, "What Does It Mean to Be AAPI? 12 Young People Reflect on Their Identities," *Teen Vogue*, May 19, 2021. www.teenvogue.com.
4. Erika Lee, *The Making of Asian America: A History*. New York: Simon & Schuster, 2015, p. 3.

Chapter One: Asian Immigration to the United States

5. Lee, *The Making of Asian America*, p. 59.
6. Helen Zia, *Asian American Dreams: The Emergence of an American People*. New York: Farrar, Straus & Giroux, 2000, p. 27.
7. Asia Society, "Asian Americans Then and Now: Linking Past to Present," 2022. https://asiasociety.org.
8. Tom Rea, "The Rock Springs Massacre," WyoHistory.org, November 8, 2014. www.wyohistory.org.
9. Lee, *The Making of Asian America*, p. 117.
10. V.S. McClatchy, testimony before the Committee on Immigration, US Senate, Sixty-Eighth Congress, "A Bill to Limit the Immigration of Aliens into the United States, and for Other Purposes," March 11–15, 1924. www.hawaiiinternment.org.
11. History, Art & Archives, US House of Representatives, "Immigration and Nationality Act of 1965." https://history.house.gov.
12. Katie Beck, "The Korean American Success Story," BBC, March 30, 2011. www.bbc.com.
13. Quoted in Linda Ha, "The Hmong Community: Resilience, Hope and a Place in America," ABC 7 Eyewitness News, May 10, 2021. https://abc7chicago.com.
14. Sarah Schafer, "In Their Own Words: Celebrating, but Not Feeling Celebrated, During Asian American and Pacific Islander Month," UNHCR Spotlight, May 24, 2021. www.unhcr.org.

Chapter Two: Fighting for Rights

15. Quoted in Biography, "Japanese Internment Camp Survivors: In Their Own Words," May 13, 2021. www.biography.com.
16. Madeline Hsu, "Understanding America: Asian American History, Contributions, and Current Challenges," US Department of State, May 7, 2021. www.state.gov.
17. "Nationality Act of 1790," Immigration History.https://immigrationhistory.org.
18. Cornell Law School Legal Information Institute, "*Takao Ozawa v. United States*." www.law.cornell.edu.

19. Cornell Law School Legal Information Institute, "*United States v. Bhagat Singh Thind*." www.law.cornell.edu.
20. Densho Encyclopedia, "Alien Land Laws," October 8, 2020. https://encyclopedia.densho.org.
21. Quoted in Densho Digital Archive, Japanese American Museum of San Jose, "Eiichi Sakauye Interview," February 8, 2005. https://encyclopedia.densho.org.
22. Equal Justice Initiative, "The Farmworkers' Movement," December 1, 2014. https://eji.org.
23. Dennis Arguelles, "Remembering the Manongs and Story of the Filipino Farm Worker Movement," National Parks Conservation Association, May 25, 2017. www.npca.org.
24. Quoted in Judith Cummings, "Detroit Asian-Americans Protest Lenient Penalties for Murder," *New York Times*, April 26, 1983. www.nytimes.com.
25. Alex Tizon, *Big Little Man*. Boston: Houghton Mifflin Harcourt, 2014, p. 59.

Chapter Three: Creating New Communities

26. Anna Regina Gotuaco, "Little Manila: My Home Away from Home," *The Prattler*, December 7, 2021. www.prattleronline.com.
27. Library of Congress, "Immigration and Relocation in U.S. History: Taking Care of Our Own." www.loc.gov.
28. Jeff Yang et al., *Rise: A Pop History of Asian America from the Nineties to Now*. New York: Mariner, 2022, p. 49.
29. Lisa Kwon, "'Churches Are Everywhere.' How Korean Immigrants Used Religious Institutions to Create a Community in Koreatown," L.A. Taco, August 6, 2019. www.lataco.com.
30. Quoted in Kwon, "'Churches Are Everywhere.'"
31. Quoted in Turner, "The Many Asian Americas."
32. Quoted in Turner, "The Many Asian Americas."
33. Quoted in Turner, "The Many Asian Americas."
34. Lee, *The Making of Asian America*, pp. 357–58.
35. Lee, *The Making of Asian America*, pp. 361–62.
36. Lee, *The Making of Asian America*, p. 370.

Chapter Four: Embracing Identity

37. Bee Vue Yang, "My Hmong American Experience," Family Services, May 10, 2021. www.familyservicesnew.org.
38. Quoted in *New York Times*, "How It Feels to Be Asian in Today's America," September 25, 2021. www.nytimes.com.
39. Frank H. Wu, *Yellow: Race in America Beyond Black and White*. New York: Basic Books, 2002, p. 7.
40. Quoted in Yang et al., *Rise*, p. 156.
41. Quoted in Holly Corbett, "Some Truths About Being Asian in America: A Growing Voice," *Forbes*, March 30, 2021. www.forbes.com.
42. Jason J. Han, "Why I Stopped Believing in 'Putting My Head Down' and Assimilating as an Asian American," *Philadelphia Inquirer*, April 6, 2021. www.inquirer.com.
43. Han, "Why I Stopped Believing in 'Putting My Head Down' and Assimilating as an Asian American."
44. Diana Elizabeth, "Growing Up Asian American!," *Diana Elizabeth* (blog),

February 11, 2021. https://dianaelizabethblog.com.

45. Viet Tran, "'I Am a Queer Vietnamese American, but Not Always in That Order," Human Rights Campaign, June 10, 2019. www.hrc.org.

46. Sammi Wong, "How Asian-American Designers Have Impacted the Fashion Industry," Excuse My Thoughts, May 25, 2021. https://excusemythoughts.com.

47. Ligaya Mishan, "Asian-American Cuisine's Rise, and Triumph," *New York Times*, November 10, 2017. www.nytimes.com.

48. Vishakha N. Desai, "Are You American Enough? Reflections on Being an Asian in America," Asian Society, April 1, 2021. https://asiasociety.org.

49. Selina Wang, "Too Chinese for the US, Too American for China. Where Can Asian Americans like Me Call Home?," CNN, April 10, 2021. www.cnn.com.

50. Quoted in Charlé LaMonica, "Asian American Experiences," UNC World View, April 9, 2021. https://worldview.unc.edu.

51. Quoted in LaMonica, "Asian American Experiences."

Chapter Five: Ongoing Challenges

52. Quoted in Eric Lee and Marco Storel, "Asian American Teens Navigate Being Themselves as Their Communities Are Targeted," NPR, October 17, 2021. www.npr.org.

53. Quoted in Colby Itkowitz, "Trump Uses Racially Insensitive Term to describe Coronavirus," *Washington Post*, June 23, 2020. www.washingtonpost.com.

54. Shirin Sinnar, written statement submitted to the US House Committee on the Judiciary Subcommittee on the Constitution, Civil Rights, and Civil Liberties for a Hearing on "Discrimination and Violence Against Asian Americans," March 18, 2021. https://docs.house.gov.

55. Yang et al., *Rise*, p. 420.

56. Zia, *Asian American Dreams*, p. 9.

57. Elizabeth, "Growing Up Asian American."

58. Quoted in Christine Ro, "The Docility Myth Flattening Asian Women's Careers," BBC, August 16, 2020. www.bbc.com.

59. Amber Ly, "How 'Positive' Stereotypes Hurt Asian-Americans Like Me," YR Media, June 22, 2016. https://yr.media.

60. Quoted in Ly, "How 'Positive' Stereotypes Hurt Asian-Americans Like Me."

61. Quoted in Richard Morgan, "Asian American Masculinity Is Being Increasingly Celebrated. But Many Men Still Face Stereotyping," *Washington Post*, June 22, 2021. www.washingtonpost.com.

62. Mallika Kallingal, "These Asian Americans Faced Racism Growing Up, but They Won't Let It Define Them," CNN, March 27, 2021. www.cnn.com.

63. Quoted in *Allure*, "I'm Done Downplaying My Asian American Experience," February 14, 2021. www.allure.com.

64. USC Pacific Asia Museum, "Debunking the Model Minority Myth." https://pacificasiamuseum.usc.edu.

65. Lee, *The Making of Asian America*, p. 376.

66. Quoted in Li Zhou, "The Inadequacy of the Term 'Asian American,'" Vox, May 5, 2021. www.vox.com.

67. Zhou, "The Inadequacy of the Term 'Asian American.'"

68. Lee, *The Making of Asian America*, pp. 391–92.

FOR FURTHER RESEARCH

Books

Coalition of Asian Pacifics in Entertainment, *My Life: Growing Up Asian in America*. New York: Pocket, 2022.

Lan Dong, ed., *25 Events That Shaped Asian American History: An Encyclopedia of the American Mosaic*. Santa Barbara, CA: Greenwood, 2019.

Jeff Yang et al., *Rise: A Pop History of Asian America from the Nineties to Now*. New York: Mariner, 2022.

David K. Yoo and Eiichiro Azuma, eds., *The Oxford Handbook of Asian American History*. New York: Oxford University Press, 2020.

Paula Yoo, *From a Whisper to a Rallying Cry: The Killing of Vincent Chin and the Trial That Galvanized the Asian American Movement*. New York: Norton Young Readers, 2021.

Internet Sources

Abby Budman and Neil G. Ruiz, "Key Facts About Asian Americans: A Diverse and Growing Population," Pew Research Center, April 29, 2021. www.pewresearch.org.

Madeline Hsu, "Understanding America: Asian American History, Contributions, and Current Challenges," US Department of State, May 7, 2021. www.state.gov.

New York Times, "How It Feels to Be Asian in Today's America," September 25, 2021. www.nytimes.com.

Nina Strochlic, "America's Long History of Scapegoating Its Asian Citizens," *National Geographic*, September 2, 2020. www.nationalgeographic.com.

Olivia B. Waxman and Paulina Cachero, "11 Moments from Asian American History That You Should Know," *Time*, April 30, 2021. https://time.com.

Websites

Asian American Education Project
https://asianamericanedu.org
The Asian American Education Project works to educate people about the experiences of Asian Americans. Its website contains numerous short lessons for students about the experiences of Asian Americans throughout history.

Asia Society
https://asiasociety.org
The Asia Society works to achieve peace, freedom, and prosperity for Asia and the world. It does this by encouraging dialogue and a sharing of diverse viewpoints. The Asia Society website includes numerous articles related to being Asian American.

Stop AAPI Hate
https://stopaapihate.org
The Stop AAPI Hate coalition tracks and responds to incidents of hate and discrimination against Asian Americans and Pacific Islanders in the United States. Its website has numerous statistics about hate and discrimination experienced by Asian Americans.

US Department of Health and Human Services Office of Minority Health
https://minorityhealth.hhs.gov
The US Department of Health and Human Services Office of Minority Health works to improve the health of racial and ethnic minority populations, including Asian Americans. Its website contains numerous facts about the Asian population in the United States.

INDEX

Note: Boldface page numbers indicate illustrations.

Agricultural Workers Organizing Committee (AWOC), 26, **26**
Ahmed, Sara, 50
alien land laws, 23–24, 25
architecture, 43–44
Arguelles, Dennis, 26
Aromatherapy Spa (Atlanta, Georgia), 47
Asian American Dreams (Zia), 10
Asian American Political Alliance, 41
Asian Americans
    binary identity of, **45**, 45–46
    focus on race of, 39
    growing up in White communities, 33–35
    most decorated combat unit in US military history and, 24
    origin of term, 41
    resentment over being different and attempts to distance from heritage and, 38, 39–41
Asian Pacific American Heritage Month, 32
Asian(s)
    as biologically different and inferior than Americans, 21
    as defined by US Census Bureau, 6–7
    as percentage of all immigrants, 1901–1920 and 1980–1993, 15
    as percentage of unauthorized immigrants, 7
    on teaching about, in America, 24

Asia Society, 11

Bach, Bernard, 51
Basu, Diksha, 6
Beck, Katie, 16
Bhatia, Sabeer, 42–43
birthright citizenship, 22–23

California
    Alien Land Law (1913), 23–24
    Chinatown in San Francisco, 30, **34**, 37
    Filipino Americans enclave in Los Angeles, 32
    percentage of Asian Americans in, 33
Cambodian refugees from Khmer Rouge, 16
Cato Institute, 19
Center for Immigration Studies, 15
Center for the Study of Hate & Extremism, 47–48
Chavez, Cesar, 26
Chen, Steven, 42, **43**
Chin, Vincent, 27–28, **28**
"Chinatown Resource Guide" (PBS), 37
Chinese Exclusion Act (1882), 12
Chinese immigrants
    early jobs of, 10–11, 12, **12**
    first woman, 17
    in Hawaii, 11
    as largest immigrant group, **5**, 7
    laws targeting, 11–12, 14
    population (1870), 10
    Rock Springs, Wyoming, riot and, 12–13
Choi, Cynthia, 32
Chu, Steven, 40
Chung, Nicole, 6, 33–34
citizenship
    dual, 36

    land ownership and, 24–25
    Supreme Court decisions about, 21–23
civil rights organizations
    Asian American Political Alliance, 41
    Stop AAPI Hate, 32, 47
contributions of Asian Americans, 42–45, **43**
countries of origin
    of largest number of recent immigrants, 19
    as percentage of Asian American population, **5**, 7
courts, testifying in, 12
COVID-19, 47–49
Craig, Tina Chen, 52–53

Daly City, California, 29
Delano Grape Strike (1965), **26**, 26–27
demographics, 4
Densho Encyclopedia (website), 23–24
Desai, Vishakha N., 45
discrimination. *See* racism

education
    academic achievement stereotype, 51, **52**
    degrees held, 4
Elizabeth, Diana, 42, 50
Equal Justice Initiative, 25
ethnic communities
    Chinatowns, 30, **34**, 37
    Filipino American, 29, **31**, 32
    importance of, 29, 31
    locations of, 32–33
    in western US, 33

farmworker rights, 25–27, **26**
fashion, 44
Filipino Americans enclaves, 29, **31**, 32

61

Filipino Cultural School, 32
Filipino immigrants as farm
    laborers, 25–27
food, **36**, 44–45
Fourteenth Amendment (US
    Constitution), 23
Frydman, Jonathan, 8

Gee, Emma, 41
Gotuaco, Anna Regina, 29
government, Asian
    Americans in, 27

Han, Jason J., 41–42
Harris, Kamala, 27
hate crimes
    COVID-19 and, 47–49
    increase in number of,
        47–48
    killings at Aromatherapy
        Spa in Atlanta, 47
    protests against, **49**
Hawaii
    Chinese immigrants in, 11
    as home to Asian
        Americans, 33
    Japanese immigrants
        in, 19
History, Art & Archives
    (website of US House of
    Representatives), 15
Hmong immigrants
    culture, **39**
    Vietnam War and, 17–18,
        18
Hotmail, 42–43
Hsu, Madeline, 21
Hurley, Chad, 42, **43**

Ichioka, Yuji, 41
immigration
    changing basis of, 14–15,
        15
    laws limiting, 12, 14
Immigration Act (1924), 14
Immigration and
    Naturalization Act (1965),
    14–15, **15**
income, 5, 54–55
Indian Americans, **5**, 7, **8**

Japanese Americans
    as farmers, 13–14

internment of mainland,
    during World War II, 19,
    20–21, **22**
population on mainland
    (1942), 20
Japanese immigrants
    early, 13, 32
    in Hawaii, 19
    laws limiting, 14
John F. Kennedy Presidential
    Library and Museum, 43
Johnson, Akemi, 34

Kallingal, Mallika, 51–52
Karim, Jawed, 42, **43**
Kaye, Liann, 53
Khmer Rouge, 16
Kim, Daniel Dae, 24
Kim, Ron, 16
Kim, SeoJun, 16
Kim, Sunhee, 16
Korean immigrants
    adoption of, 6
    enclaves of, 32–33
    increase in and change
        in profession of
        immigrants after 1965
        immigration act, 15–16
Kwon, Lisa, 32–33

land ownership, 23–25
Laos, refugees from, 16
laws
    changing basis of
        immigration, 14–15, **15**
    limiting immigration, 12,
        14
    targeting Chinese
        immigrants, 11–12
Lee, Cha Fong, 17–18
Lee, Eric, 48
Lee, Erika
    on importance of Asian
        Americans to US, 55
    on Japanese American
        farmers, 13–14
    on living transnationally,
        35, 37
    on "model minority"
        stereotype, 54
    on significant similarities
        among Asian
        Americans, 9

Li, Grace Z., 17
Library of Congress, 19, 30
life expectancy, 4
Lim, Geraldine, 39
Lin, Maya, 43–44
Little Manila in Queens, New
    York City, 29, **31**
Los Angeles, ethnic
    communities in, 32–33
Ly, Amber, 51

*Making of Asian America,
    The: A History* (Lee), 9
McClatchy, V.S., 14
Microsoft Outlook, 42–43
Migration Policy Institute,
    15, 19
Mishan, Ligaya, 44–45
Moy, Afong, 17
Myanmar, Rohingya refugees
    from, 18

National Farm Workers
    Association, 26, **26**
Naturalization Act (1790), 21
New York Times
    (newspaper), 44–45
Nguyen, Amanda, 44
Nguyen, Eric, 6

Oregon, 23
Ozawa, Takao, 21–22

Pacific Islanders, 27
pan-Asian awareness, 28
Park, Jeong, 51
Park, Rhea, 51
Patel, Dipa, 35
Patel, Pratik, 35
Peterson, Elliott, 47
Peterson, Robert, 47
Pew Research Center
    countries of origin of
        largest groups of Asian
        immigrants, 7
    incomes of Asian
        Americans, 54–55
    increase in number of hate
        crimes against Asians,
        47–48
    percentage of immigrants
        unauthorized, 7
    residences of Asian
        Americans, 33

Pham, Tiffany, 52
population
  countries of origin of Asian American population, **5**, 7
  countries of origin of largest number of recent immigrants, 19
  percentage of, Asian Americans and Pacific Islanders, 27
  states with largest, **5**
  total Asian, 4, 7

racism
  acceptance of heritage and, 41–42
  alien land laws, 23–24
  assumptions others make and, 38–39
  COVID-19 and, 47–49
  early Chinese immigrants and, 10–13
  early Japanese immigrants and, 14
  internment of mainland Japanese Americans during World War II, 19, 20–21, **22**
  organizations fighting Asian American Political Alliance, 41
    Stop AAPI Hate and, 32, 47
  sentence for murder of Chin, 27–28, **28**
  Trump and, 48–49
  See also hate crimes; stereotypes
Reflective Democracy Campaign, 27
refugees
  camps in Thailand for Southeast Asian Hmong, 17
  Rohingya from Myanmar, 18
  from war and violence, 16
Rise, 44
Rise: A Pop History of Asian America from the Nineties to Now (Jeff Yang, Phil Yu, and Philip Wang), 49
Rock & Roll Hall of Fame and Museum, 43

Rock Springs, Wyoming, riot, 12–13
Rohingya refugees from Myanmar, 18

Sadasivam, Krishna M., 40
Sakauye, Eiichi, 25
Sexual Assault Survivors' Rights Act (2016), 44
Simmons, Kimora Lee, 44
Sinnar, Shirin, 49
Song, Young Soo, 33
stereotypes
  academic achievement, 51, **52**
  could not be born in US, 50
  men as not athletic or good looking, 51
  "model minority," 53–55
  passivity, 50
  reactions to, 51–53
  women as sex objects, 53
Stop AAPI Hate, 32, 47
Sui, Anna, 44
Suong, Sarath, 55

Tang, Emma, 48
technology, 42–43, **43**
Thind, Bhagat Singh, 22
Tizon, Alex, 28
Tong, William, 27
Tran, Viet, 42
transcontinental railroad, 10–11, **12**
transnationalism, 35–37, **36**
Trump, Donald, 48–49
Tsukamoto, Mary, 20
Turner, Karen, 6, 33

unauthorized immigrants, 7
United Farm Workers (UFW), 26, **26**
United Nations High Commissioner for Refugees (UNHCR), 16, 18
US Census Bureau, 6–7
US Constitution, 23
USC Pacific Asia Museum, 53
US Supreme Court
  decision about alien land laws, 25

decisions about Asian citizenship, 21–23

Vietnam and Vietnam War, refugees from, 16, 17–18, **18**
Vietnam Veterans Memorial (Washington DC), 43–44

Wang, Alexander, 44
Wang, Philip, 49
Wang, Selina, 46
Wang, Vera, 44
women
  murder at Aromatherapy Spa of, 47
  as sex objects, 53
  sexual assault laws and, 44
Wong, Sammy, 44
Wong Kim Ark, 23
World Trade Center (original), 43
World War II
  internment of mainland Japanese Americans, 19, 20–21, **22**
  Japanese immigrants in Hawaii, 19
  most decorated combat unit in US military history, 24
Wu, Frank H., 39
Wu, Jason, 44
Wyoming State Historical Society (website), 12–13

Yamasaki, Minoru, 43
Yang, Bee Vue, 38
Yang, Jeff, 31, 49
You, Sam, 38–39
YouTube, 42, **43**
Yu, Phil, 49
Yue, Yong Ae, 47

Zhou, Li, 55
Zia, Helen
  on Chinese and building of Transcontinental Railroad, 10–11
  on stereotyping of Asian Americans, 50
  on teaching about Asians in America, 24

PICTURE CREDITS

Cover: iStock and Shutterstock

4: aelitta/iStock (top right)
Pie: Maury Aaseng
Li Chaoshul/Shutterstock.com (bottom left)
LightField Studios/Shutterstock.com (bottom right)
5: Maury Aaseng: chart and map
Iyikon/Shutterstock.com (middle)
8: RAMNIKLAL MODI/Shutterstock.com
12: Everett Collection/Newscom
15: Abaca Press/Alamy Stock Photo
18: Associated Press
22: American Photo Archive/Alamy Stock Photo
26: Associated Press
28: ZUMA Press Inc/Alamy Stock
31: Richard Levine/Alamy Stock Photo
34: eddie-hernandez.com/Shutterstock.com
36: Patti McConville/Alamy Stock Photo
39: Roberto Galan/Shutterstock.com
43: ZUMA Press, Inc./Alamy Stock Photo
45: Sorapop Udomsri/Shutterstock.com
49: Sheila Fitzgerald/Shutterstock.com
52: Tom Wang/Shutterstock.com
54: franckreporter/iStock

Sources: Asian Americans by the Numbers
- Nicolas Jones, et all., "2019: 1-Year Estimates Selected Population Profiles, American Community Survey," US Census Bureau, 2019. https://data.census.gov.
- US Department of Health and Human Services Office of Minority Health, "Profile: Asian Americans." www.pewresearch.org.
- Abby Budiman and Neil G. Ruiz, "Key Facts About Asian Origin Groups in the U.S.," *Pew Research Center*, April 29, 2021. www.pewresearch.org.
- US Department of Health and Human Services Office of Minority Health, "Profile: Asian Americans." www.pewresearch.org.
- US Department of Health and Human Services Office of Minority Health, "Profile: Asian Americans." www.pewresearch.org.
- Abby Budiman and Neil G. Ruiz, "Key Facts About Asian Origin Groups in the U.S."